"CAPTAIN JACK" AND THE SONGS OF BLACK SLADE OFF THE LINE.

Wiley Whitfield Jr.

STUDIO OF BOOKS
THE SPACE FOR YOUR MESSAGE

Studio of Books LLC
5900 Balcones Drive Suite 100
Austin, Texas 78731
www.studioofbooks.org
Hotline: (254) 800-1183

Ordering Information:
Special discounts are available on quantity purchases by corporations, associations, and others. For details, contact the publisher at the address above.

Printed in the United States of America.

ISBN-13: Softcover   978-1-964864-54-9
          Ebook   978-1-964864-55-6

Library of Congress Control Number: 2024918852

DEDICATION

First, giving honor to "God" and to my mother and father, Evelyn and Wile Whitfield Sr. This book is also dedicated to my grandmother "Lillie" and the blood of the Cherokee.

I would like to dedicate this book to The International Fellowship of Christians and Jews. Also, PETA People for the Ethical Treatment of Animals and Mercy Ships.

I would also like to dedicate this book to Evelyn Diekhaus, who at the young age of 9, perished while trying to save lives of others as she tried to pull the fire alarm. I recommend that she be awarded with the Medal Of Honor to applaud her bravery.

FOREWORD

This is not a "colored book." This is a 'black face' book with white writing for the benefit of those who love to distinguish a difference. I will always remember my educated teacher who would say he was a "cute" little black boy… and I knew my black crayolas were nothing like the color of my skin… I would ask myself, where did this lie begin? This lie about the color of skin. I was about ten. It even offended me, then. As a theme for this book, I have chosen "anger management," within poetic expressions, by a country boy.

Contents

Introduction

"THE SONGS OF BLACK SLADE... OFF THE LINE."

The Assembly line, where I am employed with Daimler Chrysler in Fenton, MO. I began writing songs whenever I had time to spare, on my breaks. If there is an underlying theme to this book, it would be my attempted poetic expression as to why "I" believe in God. I wrote this compilation of poems to entertain and to share with you some of my most profound experiences.

While in the Arm, I was fortunate to be able to travel and see other countries. At one time, I was fluent in five languages. Many of my poems talk about the military way of life. I like to say that my poetry is flavored with the blues because many times, I am inspired to write when I have blues playing in the background, country western, and religious music also. "The Songs of Black Slade, Off the Line"... Poems of Mine

Thank you, Mrs. Hunter Bodkins, for your diligent effort put into typing my manuscript.

About the Author

I was raised on a farm — with eleven children and in a religious family. After high school, I entered the military. I traveled through Italy, Germany, Korea, and Japan. And I have written songs about these lands.

I would be stupid if I didn't believe in the 'Almighty' because he has shown me many signs. I can't even count them all. For example, he showed me four signs in four different countries in the world. I believe it's divine how these events occurred. He physically positioned me in these countries at precisely the right time in order to be able to physically save someone's life. The 'devil' wanted them to die, and the 'Almighty' used me to keep it from happening.

THEME

"Believe in God and …
Believe in Kickin' …
When it's time!"

TWO CAPTAINS

They both have the same name
and the same red head band;
the same black pearl ring on
their right hand.
They both wear a gold tooth and...
a cut-off HANGMAN'S NOOSE!
Wiley Whitfield Jr. "Captain Jack"
Pirate of the Caravans 30 Nov. 2000, photocopy modified
"The Songs of Black Slade… Off the Line"
Johnny Dcpp
Belleville New Democrat
11 July 2003
"Captain Jack" — "Pirates of the Caribbean"
Wiley Whitfield Jr.
5-12-2000
From Captain Jack and the Songs of
Black Slade Off the Line.

Identity Theft

I was in my I was sitting at my kitchen table writing, the Tv was on, and I heard the announcer say, "There's a new movie being released today! With the title of: "Pirates of the Caribbean." I didn't look up. I continued writing. And then he said it would be starring Johnny Depp as the flamboyant "Captain Jack." At this time, I had to look up for two reasons, "Captain Jack" has been my nickname for over thirty years, and Johnny Depp has always been one of my favorite actors.

The next thing he said is that "Captain Jack" wears a red headband and has a gold tooth! I thought about my years while I worked on the assembly line. The gold tooth I have worn since my first tour of military duty in 1964. This was the most amazing series of coincidences I had ever seen. At this time, I was compelled to go see the movie. The next day the Belleville New Democrat released some additional information about the movie. Ironically Johnny Depp stated to the newspaper that he chose to do the role of "Captain Jack" because he wanted to get away from "the assembly line" way of making movies! Well, Mr. Depp, I am "Captain Jack," and I work on the assembly line for Daimler Chrysler in Fenton, MO. It appears that my identity has been taken off the line, and it appears that someone is lyin'. Three years ago, I decided what I wanted to use on the cover of my first book of poetry. I decided to take an old photograph of mine taken at a time when I was in my prime. It was in black and white, so I modified it to a degree with a band around my head, in "Captain Jack" and the Songs of Black Slade…Off the Line.

The color of red. This explains why I was surprised to see Johnny Depp's picture as "Captain Jack" in the Belleville News-Democrat. On 11 July 2003, his picture looked like me! to a degree!

The first week I started working for Chrysler in Fenton, Mo, on the second shift. I was walking through the gate when someone called me "Captain Jack"! When I turned around, I saw a man I had never met before. I asked him why did he call me by that name when he had never met me before? He said, "I called you that because you look like "Captain Jack."" His name was Francis, a Vietnam vet.

I went to see the movie "Pirates of the Caribbean." After seeing this movie, I have come to believe that my identity has been stolen from me off the line. I think it is unfair. I began listing the similarities taken off the line.

I was given the name Captain Jack in 1964, and I got my gold tooth while on military duty.

For years I have worn a red headband on the line, and I have worn my black pearl ring for five years in time. His ring is a copy of mine!

The movie "Elizabeth" is the main focus. Also for me, my grandbaby, who is named "Elizabeth," is my main focus.

Five years ago, I dedicated a poem to her explaining how I received the name "Captain Jack."

Wiley Whitfield Jr. November 2004.

Identity Theft – Part II

I believe I am the victim of a certain kind of Identity Theft. This activity has been done by Walt Disney Productions and Johnny Depp.

My story began, it was on 10 Jul. 2003. I was sitting at my kitchen table, and the TV was on. I heard the announcer say, "There is a new movie being released today. Its title is Pirates of the Caribbean and the Curse of the Black Pearl." I didn't look up, and then he said, "It will be starring Johnny Depp as the flamboyant Captain Jack! At this time, I had to look up for two reasons: number one, Johnny Depp has always been one of my favorite actors since he first starred in 21 Jump Street, and Captain Jack has been my nickname for over thirty years. This was the first coincidence.

The next thing the announcer said was that Captain Jack wears a Read Head Band, and he wears a gold tooth! This was the second and third coincidence, I also wear a Red Head Band, and I have worn my Gold Tooth for over thirty years. The Read Head Band I have worn for nine years where I work.

At this point in time, I was compelled to go see the movie. The next day, the newspaper made the same announcement about the movie being released. They interviewed Mr. Johnny Depp, and they asked him why did he choose to play the role of Captain Jack? He stated that he wanted to do something different from the "Assembly Line" way of making movies he had been doing in the past. This was the fourth coincidence. I presently work on an "Assembly Line." I work for Daimler Chrysler in Fenton, Mo, second shift…

Five years ago, I designed the cover for my first book of poetry, I used an old black and white photograph of myself, and I modified the photo by sketching a redhead bank on it. In the photo, I am holding my right hand up to my chin… This was the fifth coincidence; the newspaper displayed a picture of Johnny Depp as Captain Jack… It is the same picture pose as the one I designed for my book.

I went to see the movie, and after seeing the movie… 15 additional coincidences were noted from the screen and the DVD cover.

Coincidences #6, #7, #8

With the use of a magnifying glass, I came to realize that the Red headband is more than just a Red headband. Under close scrutiny, I could see that the design within both headbands is basically the same. It shows two points pointing in the direction of each other in the center of the headband. I considered this to be coincidence #6.

In back reference to the newspaper photo, in addition to the headband and the hand touching the chin in both photos, there also appears to be a similarity in the hairline, as coincidence #7.

I published a poem five years ago through the International Library of Poetry. It was a poem that explained how I received the "Captain Jack" name. The company sent me a wall plaque with the poem printed on a "scroll." Coincident #8. Walt Disney Productions is also using a "scroll" to display the title of the movie on the DVD cover.

Coincidences #9 and #10

Coincidence #9

On the DVD cover, the scroll has located in its top left-hand corner a small picture of a skull… In the same corner on my scroll, it too contains a small picture. It is one of a flower bouquet, but when I examined it through the use of a magnifying magnifying glass, the flowers converted to a picture of a face.

To this end, Coincidence #10

The ring. I have worn my black pearl ring for about five years in time while I work on the line, and on the DVD cover, Mr. Depp's ring even looks like mine: a black pearl encircled in a black and white design.

Coincidences #11 and #12

In this letter, I will try to explain what I consider to be #11 and #12 in the line of coincidences. I will try to make you see what I saw after a one-time viewing of the movie. For many years, I have been known for wearing wristbands. There are several styles that one can wear. For the last (approximately) 10 years, I have been wearing the black wrap-around kind. They are especially unique in that they have a thumb strap attached.

When I saw the movie, I could see that his wrist was wrapped with black bands. When I saw the DVD cover for the movie… It shows that the wristbands have attached to them a thumb strap.

Coincidences #13, #14, #15

I find it to be coincidental that both Captains rely on the use of a gun in their line of work. My gun at work is a type of ratchet drill that shoots screws. I am the only person on the line where I work that uses this type of drill. It is referred to as a gun, and it is also connected to a universal joint that can allow the gun to be rotated in any direction necessary to shoot screws.

In the movie and on the DVD cover, it shows that Johnny Depp's gun looks very similar in shape and basic appearance to mine. His gun also shows that a universal joint is also attached. We both see guns in our work. The guns are similar in appearance. Both guns have a universal joint attached.

Coincidences #16,

THE HANGMAN'S NOOSE

I wear a unique necklace; it is a replica of a Hangman's Noose. It is made from an old black shoestring. Some years ago, I wrote a short story about a little boy who found his dad hanging from a tree one day as he was walking through the woods. He wanted to get his dad down, but he was too small to do it. He couldn't reach high enough, so he couldn't get him down. He was able to reach his dad's feet, so he took one shoestring to keep. He tied it around his neck lose like a noose. It was to be a reminder to him in time for whoever had done this crime.

In the final scene of the movie "Pirates of the Caribbean." Captain Jack has been captured, and he is about to be hanged. At the gallows, the hangman's noose is around his neck… Miraculously someone cuts the rope just in time, and Captain Jack is saved: He still has the cut-off hangman's noose still around his neck. So as coincidence #16, we are both wearing a cut-off HANGMAN's NOOSE.

Coincidences #17,

THE GOLD MEDALLION

We are both wearing a gold medallion. I have worn mine for five years; I wear the medallion around my neck on a gold chain. Johnny Depp is also wearing a gold medallion that looks very similar to the one I wear. He wears it attached to his headband. There is an inscription on my medallion; I believe there is an inscription on the medallion that Johnny Depp is wearing, and I believe that the two may be the same, and if so, this would be an additional coincidence to explain.

Coincidences #18,

THE DVD COVER

When I designed the cover for my first book of poetry approximately five years ago, I chose to use an old black and white photograph modified with the sketch of a red headband on the picture. White lettering against a black background.

The DVD cover for this movie shows a black label with white lettering and a skull in black and white with a red headband. The covers are basically the same.

Coincidences #19,

THE SASHAY

This particular coincidence can only be described as a dance. When I work on the assembly line for hours and hours of walking back and forth in a short space, I sometimes use little dance steps and turns to help motivate myself through the monotonous repetitions of the job.

In the movie, Johnny Depp chose to specifically use an unusual dance sashay at different times throughout the movie.

The crew on board the ship is working on a line similar to an assembly line.

Coincidences #20,

WIL AND KIERA

In this coincidence, the other two stars and named Wil and Kiera. I see a coincidence in the fact that Wil is short for my first name, which is Wiley, or it can be spelled as Wily. The name Kiera is short for Kieral or Carol, which is the same first name as that of my wife.

Coincidences #21,

THE LAST COMMERCIAL

After seeing the movie once, I recorded all of these coincidences. Approximately a week or two after, I happened to be watching the TV at just the right time to see Johnny Depp in his latest commercial promoting his next movie. In this short commercial, he appeared to be some type of military officer in charge of a prison, and he seemed to be interrogating a certain prisoner. He seemed to be threatening the prisoner for writing a certain book!

The coincidence here is that I, too, am writing a book, and there are some who may want it discontinued.

Coincidences #22,

THE NINTH GATE

About a month after seeing the movie, I randomly selected a book to read from my bookcase. For a few moments, I pondered over the Harvard Classics lined up on the shelf before I decided which one to pick. I decided to take the very last book on the shelf. I pulled it down and opened it to the first page…It was the story of Don Quixote of the Mancha by Miguel de Cervantes.

The next day I was watching the TV, and a movie was starting to play starring Johnny Depp. The movie begins in a college classroom, and the book being studied is Don Quixote of the Mancha. The title of the movie is Ninth Gate.

Coincidences #23,

THE SECRET WINDOW

The next movie that Johnny Depp appeared in was titled "The Secret Window." In this movie, he plays the part of a writer who is accused of stealing literary work from another. It is a coincidence that I am making the same accusation.

Coincidences #24,

TO BE A WRITER

I was up late one night watching the TV; someone was interviewing Johnny Depp. He was sitting on stage, and the audience was made up of college students. They were asking him questions. He was asked what he would like to be doing if he was not an actor. He replied that he wanted to be a writer. What a coincidence, I am a writer, one addicted to the process of thought recordation.

Coincidences #25,

ELIZABETH

Last but not least. In the movie, Captain jack is on a destiny mission or a quest to save ELIZABETH, which is his main focus throughout the movie. The irony and coincidence here is the fact that I, too, am on a mission or quest to save Elizabeth. She is my granddaughter, and she is my main focus. She is caught in the middle of a struggle between me and my son, a brilliant criminal attorney on the run.

A TRIBUTE…
TO ELIZABETH,
ALEXANDRIA, SEOUL,
KYLE, AND JOSHUA

Grandaddy? What did you do in the Army? What was your trade? Baby, your granddaddy went from "Private" to "Captain Jack" to "Sergeant Major, Jack Slade," …and I never got paid. And I did not have it made… in no shade. You see, they started calling me "Captain jack" after a "drill sergeant" kicked me, and I didn't fight him back. Can you understand why I didn't fight back? I didn't fight back because I had a 'flashback' to a time when my daddy had killed a man for the same reason as that and… I didn't want to do that.

So, I looked at that "drill," and my heart was pounding to kill, and it was not God's will. So, I smiled and got myself up off the ground, I didn't look mad, and I didn't even frown, and after that, they started calling me Captain Jack.

So, you see, the secret to growing old is to always do as you are told.

A lot of kids don't do what their parents say, and that's why some are dead today.

Always do whatever your mom and daddy say.

A Settlement Solution

TO MR. JOHNNY DEPP & DISNEY PRODUCTIONS

I, too, am concerned about the legacy I leave for my grandchildren, the same honorable concern that Johnny Depp had for his grandchildren. I believe I am entitled to a fair share of the production of this movie.

I don't have any legal advisers, and I don't have the kind of money required to fight in court over possible copyright infringements on the "Captain Jack."

If my request is unreasonable, it appears to me that this settlement can be made between Johnny Depp and everyone to see. An old fashion fistfight, no guns, no knives, no broken bones… and no sticks and stones. If I win, I get my name back and my share of "Captain Jack." If I lose, sir, this will allow me the honor to show my grandchildren how I fought for my name. I think I still have a fight or two in this game.

I cannot have my grandchildren thinking that I was trying to be like 'you,' when it's you who's not true. This time, I have been cleared to fight back without interference from a 'flashback'…to stop my attack.

—"Captain Jack."

The 'DC' Sembly Line Blues

The DC Sembly Line Blues can be country western, the blues, or whatever you choose, you can use. Sometimes you can feel bad, sad, or just plain old blue. It's true. Well, it's all up to you. Me, I like the blues. I've always liked the blues, especially the "DC Sembly Line Blues."

To our customers, I would like to say thanks to you and tell you a little about what we do, and that's fine because it's all about time and how we work on the line in order to build this van. That is so fine! Of course, like with any job, you can sometimes get the blue. With me, sometimes it can start with my shoes. When I've got an ear of corn in my shoes and steady-dropping screws, that can really give me the blues! Country western blues are whatever I choose, I can use.

Now, let's get back to this van on the line, "The DC Sembly Line," where it is so perfected, all wires connected and each one tested, right on the line.

You see, we put in a lot of time, a lot of sweat, grit, and grime on this line, doing our time, in order to build this van that's so fine. We dedicate ourselves to putting in the time. Everyone must do their jobs right! All screws must be torqued and tight. All wire connections are locked to perfection for your protection! You see, we strive to be the best, so our vans will pass any test. That is our quest! Here on the line, the "DC Sembly Line."

Now when the line moves, we all get in a groove and sometimes get the blues, but our pay is fine. That's why we like the line. Some people like diamonds, and some…a blackpearls… "We intend to be the premier manufacturing company in the world." Never before by mankind have there been minivans built so fine, and we build them here on the line. Sometimes it gets so hot! The line just won't stop, and you are checking the clock. You think you might drop!

It's just the blues, country western blues, are whatever you choose, you can use. Now, when all the jobs and tasks are done, it's taken outside for a final test run. It's like a sunrise reflection in a glass of fine wine. This is blues on the "Line."

Now it's all up to you, what will you choose? Will you make a van that's been dedicated with hands to make it grand? This van's ride is like a glide in motion over oceans. It can take a hill, highways, and curves, but it doesn't mean much is swerving. Our customers are satisfied, and that is our pride! They know we have tried. Now you, too, can try one, take one out for a ride, and feel that pride… of the line, the "DC Sembly Line."

Pet Loves and Angels in Disguise

Lauri inspired me to write this poem. I call her an angel in disguise: she fits the description. She's a dental assistant and had just finished working on my teeth.

She said, "Wiley, you should write a song or poem about pets." I said, "Well, I've never thought too much about that before. But I'll give it a try and see what I can come up with." This is what I came up with…

I am inspired to write this poem by an angel in disguise. For weeks, I searched my mind for a direction that would be wise.

Nothing I did was working, everything I tried… not until last night… when I cried. You see I was driving home alone, and I cried all the way home.

I became overwhelmed with sadness, seeing someone's pet by the roadside. I think the little puppy was standing there just before he died.

He had walked into the left-hand lane as I was cruising in the middle. I was in a cruise, listening to the blues, and thinking about angels in disguise.

How wonderful they can be, and so wide. And the funny thing is… they don't know when they are angels from the skies, because they are angels in disguise.

When I first noticed the little puppy in my headlight beams, I was passing by him at the same time that I saw him it seems.

I made a quick swerve and checking my rear-view mirror. I could see the distant headlights on an eighteen-wheeler!

It was a good distance behind, and on the right-hand line, and for a moment that was fine, but I knew that soon, someone would be coming up that left-hand line, and they will be flying'.

At that time my eyes slowly started filling up with tears and I started crying. I was thinking about someone's little pet getting hit and dying.

Then I started thinking about my own, the five that I own, three cats and two dogs at home, with my angel in disguise alone. I cried all the way home.

It's true, and I asked myself for me and you? What can we do? What can we do? We can be more careful in the neighborhoods, when we drive through, these little pets are just as precious as you.

So, I was crying as I drove down 255, cruising in my Chrysler van at 65, and thinking of angels in disguise.

I said Lord, that little guy in in your hands, all I can do is cry for him. Don't let him die, all I can do for him is cry. I won't even wipe the tears from eyes, I'll just let 'em dry. Just don't let him die.

He was standing in the left-hand lane when I drove by. I was cruising at 65 heading for the 255 and tears were flowing down my face, I just let them dry. They were my tears for pet lovers and angels in disguise. I ask myself, is this the direction I've been trying to find? Is that why I'm crying? Because someone's little pet lovers might be dying. Maybe I'll write this poem, that pet lovers can understand, right now I'm cruising in my Chrysler minivan and I pray he's in God's hands.

Blade Slade Gunslinger for Hire

My father-in-law inspired me to write this poem. He was dying at the time... lying in his bed and staring up at the ceiling. He pointed up and said, "Look, Dorothy. Look at that little black boy. Can you see him? He's got a red bandanna on his head...." A few moments later, he was dead.

We tried to interpret his vision and understand what he said. And so, I began to write his vision in this story that came to my head. "Black Slade, Gunslinger for Hire."

Once upon a time, the year was 1829. A little black boy six or seven years old at a time. He was walking down a dusty country road... and he was crying.

He angrily kicked a small rock beside the road, where he stopped. The rock went flying high into the tall weeds nearby, and he continued to cry.

He said to himself, "I will sure be glad when my daddy comes home. I'm tired of staying with white folks while he's gone, and he's been gone too long."

His daddy had twice escaped being hung, and he was someplace on the run from a chain gang in the sun. He was an ex-slave on the run, and he didn't have a gun.

He was an ex-slave on the run to see his son. The little boy reached into his pocket and took out his red bandana. He tied it around his head and called it 'Manda.'

The white family that he lived with were friends, so he and his dad, and they were happy about Carol, the new baby they had.

He decided to take a shortcut home through the woods, and he started to sing a song the best that he could. He said, "I see a lonely cloud in your sky Lord. I sure hope you can let it rain 'cause my daddy is somewhere in the hot sun, working on a chain gang, and he can sho nuff use your rain."

That was the song the little boy sang. He sometimes carried strapped across his back, a little guitar in a gunny sack. They lived across the tracks. When he would take this shortcut through the woods, looking up at the trees made him feel good.

But on this particular day, it wasn't the same way. It was a sad day, and the memory of what he saw would never go away.

Stories had been told to him that his daddy was on the run for something he hadn't done. They said he was a slave on the run, and he didn't have a gun. And twice before he escaped being hung. He had left back home his little son.

After three days and nights on the run, the bloodhounds tracked him down, and he was hung in the hot sun.

An old black rope was tied around his throat, and he was left in the sun to choke.

The little boy made his way home, thinking of his dad, who was gone, and the white family he was left with alone.

What he saw on the way took his breath away that day. It was a shadowed figure in a tree, and it began to take a familiar form. He could see the closer he began to approach.

It was his daddy tied with that old black rope. He was dangling from a tall oak. With the rope tied tight around his throat.

The boy cried and cried, his eyes turned red, and there was a terrible pain in his head. It was a time of hatred and bloodshed.

He wanted to, in some kind of way, just get his daddy down, but there was no one to help him around.

His daddy's body hung too high for his little arms to reach. He could barely touch his feet, so he took one shoestring to keep.

He tied the string around his neck loose, like a noose, and in his mind, he made a vow that he would travel through the south.

The string would be a memory in time, in his fight against crime. He would always be ready to greet it in order to properly defeat it.

And so, as the story is told, history was made by a little boy named "Slade." He became the gunslinger, "Black Slade." Defending the homeless and helpless was his trade.

He rode a black stallion named "van" as he traveled through the land…

Twenty years later… some kids were out playing in the shade. One looked up and said, hey! Ain't that Black Slade? Over there, he's taking a paper on that wall. Ain't that him, y'all?

The other one said, "I don't know." It looks like it might be they always said he was 'Black' to see. But that guy looks "Coppertone Brown" to me. Is there a black shoestring around his neck? Can you see?

After Black Slade tacked his poster on the wall, he rode off on another call. He rode the stallion's name "Van." There wasn't 'mini' in the land, not by Chrysler at that time, there was no "Sembly" line.

In his manner of dress, he wore a long black trench, so he could sneak up on stench. They didn't know he was near; he had no fear.

Underneath the coat, he carried two pearl handle Army 45s, one for each hand, and he carried a "Chank," which they did not understand.

It hung low by his side with an old black rope tied. He had the bandana around his head. It was red.

And the black shoestring, tied around his neck loose, like a noose.

The Black Hangin' Rope Necklace

The kids ran over to see the poster to see what was said, and this is what they read:

"Help sting for the homeless, donate and nothing less, and receive this hangin'; rope necklace…to me, it's the most beautiful to see. If you wear it like a colla', you kin hear a slave 'holla' sympathize with the pain of slavery, and hear a slave 'holla' sympathize with the pain of slavery, and get this hangin' rope necklace for free! It can slide up and down, like the real thing, when worn as a necklace to be seen. It can be worn as a headband, or it can be worn betwixt the wrist and hand.

When worn, it relates to hate and loving our fellow man. It is the replica of that real rope that cut my daddy's throat. I call it "The Black Hanging' Rope" If you can relate to hate, donate. "Black Slade: gunslinger, for Hire.

The Pride of Black Slade

Being sad inside is what made him proud. He always felt sad inside, as if something just wasn't right. Was he black inside? Or white? He knew that even as a little boy, her never experienced joy. It made his pride… when he often cried.

He would say some blacks don't like me, 'cause they say I sound white, and some whites don't like me, 'cause I don't look right. He would smile and say,

When Black Slade Met a Man

His language developed when he traveled through the land. He could speak Korean, German, Italian, and Japanese. To name just a few, he spoke English too. And one day, he met a man, a man he called a friend. They talked for a while after shaking hands. And then the man reached into his pocket, and he brought out a card. He said, here, Black Slade, read it hard. The card read that he was a member of the clan. Slade put the card back into his hand…the man then said, "Slade, as God is my witness, right here and up above, y'all the first mixed couple I ever proved of."

And as they turned and he walked away, Black Slade had this to say.. he gazed into his wife's blue eyes and said, who was that man so wise? He must be an angel in disguise.

Roadkill and Gutless Mothers

At first, it was in Jasper, and in Africa, another "Black Slade." Observed someone's mother. The sad lady stood crying and looking down at the roadkill guts in the street. There were some bits and pieces of meat on the bloodstained street… her son had just been dragged and struck… by a gutless mother… in a pickup truck.

DEDICATED TO MY MOTHER,
EVELYN WHITFIELD,
AND
THE PRESERVATION OF
DOCTOR WATTS.

Kim's Accident... Off the Line

When I heard about my friend's accident, I wanted to say something that might be of help. It had been a terrible automobile accident, and they said her back was broken…she was almost killed. From my personal experiences, I try to minimize the problem first. To me, that is the first step within the healing process, and so, this poem came to mind…

Kim, I heard about your tragic accident today, and I've searched my heart for the right thing to say. It keeps telling me you will be ok.

Just take it as one of the jobs you work through every day. I see your hard work. Every day, from across the way.

That's why I can say you will be ok. You only experienced a slight setback, a 'slightly hurt' back, that will fix that…the line will pray 'til you are back.

It won't be long. This… is your prayer song.

Getting in the Hole

You hear this a lot on the line. From time to time, getting in the hole can be cold, when you've been told. And told and told, getting in the hole can be cold. And when the wife is at home, you don't hold.

It's because you work in a small space without much time, and sometimes the line can be flyin'. Use your own space and time, and stop taking mine. It's so unkind.

Captain Jack and Sergeant Major

Jack

The year was 1988, and a single tear rolled down his face… He said, "That's not a tear, sir. It's just the wind in my eye." He began to tell again the story they would always say was a lie.

This would be the last time he would try. He said he asked his teacher, "Was white folks' skin?" and she just looked at him and grinned.

He said he was about ten. He said he needed a white Crayola for his coloring book so he could color white skin, but there was none in the box back then.

He knew that midnight was black, and he could color that, and he knew his skin wasn't that, so why did she call him black?

He could see that the box had red for red and yellow for some skin, but no white was within. He said she didn't know the color of her skin now are then…

Eight years later, a water buffalo fell to the ground. It weighed 3,200 pounds as it pounded into the ground, and there was no one to hear the sound.

There was no one to see except Kowalski and me. Kowalski was pinned underneath. I had to move in quick time to keep him from dying. Sometimes I can still hear his crying. It was a death cry. It even made me cry under that Korean sky. I don't know why he wouldn't say hi just before he was about to die.

I didn't know the buffalo's weight at that time, so I reached down the blind. I grabbed hold of the ring in his nose… it was cold. I tightly gripped it, and I slowly began to lift it. When I got it up to waist-high. I said, "Crawl out, dammit, you won't die!"

The Lieutenant called him Sgt. Major Slade… He never got paid. Privates would call him Captain Jack… he didn't ask for that.

So, this time when he walked away, he said all he had to say. He didn't look back, and that's a fact. It was the end of the sergeant Major and Captain Jack.

The Transformation of Black Slade

Sometime between the 1800 and 1900, according to the yorn, "Black Slade" and "Rain" were formed…and a cartoon bounty hunter was born. The gunslinger changed his uniform…prior to entering Cockroach City, the little city that had one time been pretty…he changed the 45s to "spray cans" and had one for each hand, and the stallions became a Chrysler minivan.

According to how histories are made…the story continues with Black Slade, he who carried Raid.

He was now a Cockroach bounty hunter looking for a place in the shade. That's where the cockroaches hatched their eggs and laid.

You see, they were cockroaches in the shade, and though they had it made… but not so, said 'Slade,' he carried Raid.

A black minivan; and two cans of Raid are how this tale is made.

He leaned back in his chair and pushed away from the table…while reading the ad he had put in the paper.

He said to his wife, it looks like I am being called for again. It's another quest. It's a call from an actor who is helpless.

It was a little city that had one time been pretty, before the cockroach's crime…and what a shame. He finished his cup of coffee and began to dress.

He wore the red bandana called "Manda" and two spray cans with pearl handles, a long black trench coat and Coppertone brown shoes, and a black shoestring around his neck tied loose.

He kissed his wife goodbye and told her not to cry. I'll be back pretty soon, maybe even before non.

He headed out West for another test. His ad in the paper read: "If your home or city is infested with cockroaches, rapists, murderers, and liars, Black Slade is for hire."

For my pay and nothing less, just donate to the homeless.

Across his shoulder, he carried a little bag inside his food, his Bible, and writing pads. And the "Chank" which no one in the world ever had.

It hung low by his side and tied with a piece of black rope to the homeless; it brought hope.

He made a triple-barrel sawed-off shotgun for those special cockroaches on the run.

When Black Slade and Raid got to Cockroach City, he caught the cockroaches all by surprise…just before sunrise.

Cockroaches were creeping, sleeping, and sneaking around the town, not making a sound.

The people in the city were running away. No one wanted to stay.

The little city which was once so pretty, what a pity! The Cockroaches were now on the run! They heard that "Slade" carried three guns.

He had a "Chang-gun," and two spray cans were in his hands. His hands were fast like lightning, and he had fun with three guns.

They were two pearl handle cans with a blast of gas for the cockroaches…

One cockroach tried to crawl up the wall, his butt slipped, and it was a terrible fall. He fell to the floor, and Raid caught him at the door.

Cockroaches were lying cryin' and dyin'. Slade and Raid was their name, and a lying cockroach was fair game.

That's how they got their fame, and it was no shame. And it was no joke for a cockroach. Slade would make them choke.

There was one they 'calt' the cockroach queen, the gull was evil, and the gull was mean. A cockroach queen.

She tried to crawl into a hole and hide, but her head was too tall and her butt was too wide, she got stuck and cried til she died.

The people in the city are now happy here. They no longer live in fear.

There's not a cockroach in town. If you see one, write his name down. When we catch him time, we can make him do time, and the pretty little city won't be crying. Raid will leave them dying.

A gas blast for trash will square away his…

It doesn't matter, be it black or white. A dead cockroach is right.

So ends another tale off the line about a man who travels through time. Don't ever run, call 911. If you see a crime, get the police on the line.

And the pretty little city won't be cryin'.

"Blade Slade"

CAROL AND THE LORAC OF GIBRALTAR

The word 'Carol' becomes 'Lorac" when you turn it back. It can also be 'low rock.' That's what this poem is about, a low rock in the road where I stopped.

I kicked the low rock in the road where I stopped. Dr. Martin Luther King, he had a dream too. The color of skin didn't bother him. Why did it bother you?

They fired me after I took Carol to the company convention. My manager said it was because we embarrassed the VIPs to see a mixed couple, and they weren't pleased with the VIPs.

It was a grand celebration. With the many Chesire cat grins when we walked in, and for my friend and me, it was the end.

I was the leading agent in the land. Out of thirty thousand, I worked the Ghetto for the high rock, but it was a low rock when they told me to stop, "Carol" and the "Lorac."

DEDICATED TO THE MEMORY OF
CAROLYN WHITAKER
LAFAYETTE GRADE SCHOOL
"THE BADGE OF AUTHORITY"

The Badge of Authority

I was a new kid in a white school, and I could see the teacher's eyes, looking around…

I got scared and started writing, with my head lowered down…

And then, when I looked up again to see, she was looking straight at me.

She pointed her finger and said, Wiley, the principal, we have to see. Come with me.

The other kids in the sixth-grade room, they knew that I was doomed.

I said, yes, ma'am and got up from my desk. I was scared and nervous and wondered what was next.

It was a long slow walk to the principal's office. We entered and closed the door…she said Wiley, we've never had a black patrol boy before… and this is your badge. You're the first this school ever had. I was so glad.

Maxine

Maine, Maxine? Maxine, why did they treat you so mean? It's because things ain't always as they seem, Maxine. You see, you were just a little black puppy, black like me, and just as cute as can be.

They put you to sleep, and that wasn't supposed to be.

You were supposed to have seven days to stay, But they kilt you the next day. What is Carol going to say?! She was crying on the phone when Sky, Kowalskn I left home, trying her best to find you a home.

After fifty calls, it didn't take her long. A newlywed couple wanted to give you that home.

I rushed back over there the next day because you now had a home and place to say. They said, "It's too late. We had to euthanize today. The black dogs go first, so the others have a place to stay, we don't have much room, so we have to do it that way. If they're black, they can't stay.

It was at the St. Clair Human Animal Control. They said you had seven days, were told. Maxine, you see, it wasn't meant to be. A dog can be the wrong color, too, in this world, you see? When you're black like me.

As Long as Long Is Long

You will hear about this song because what was done to my mother was wrong.

I will depict you in this song. You love to get the premiums and be gone.

But you won't be gone from this song. What was done to my daddy was wrong. This is his song.

I know you are bigger than me. I'm just his son, you see?

I know you have all the money and lawyers that are strong. I'll just fight with his song.

To the Mutual of Oma, I dedicated this song.

Whether it be rain, snow, sleet, or sunshine, you want the premiums on time.

Until time to pay a claim, then it's a shame, you people, with your game. My name and my dad's name are the same, and name are the same, and you owe my mother for her claim.

My mother got ripped off, and she's not the only one.

You get the premiums, and that's fun, but file a claim, and you're on the run.

You don't have it made in no shade... Black Shade.

'Twas a Buffalo Soldier and a Cold

Wall In the Sky, Kowalski

Kowalski a cold wall in the sky. Because of my skin, he wouldn't say hi. He was a cold wall in the sky and he didn't know, he was about to die. To get help I didn't have time to go, so I reached down low, and I grabbed the buffalo, by the ring that hung in his nose... it was cold, and Kowalski's cry was a death cry. He thought he would die...I lifted the buffalo 'til he was waist high. Kowalski was pinned underneath, and I couldn't let him die.

I happened in about thirty minutes time and it's been thirty-six years on my mind and I can still hear his cry sometime and over thirty years of back pain I've sustained. He was a cold wall in the sky and my military orders were divinely changed so he wouldn't die! I don't know why. I know I didn't go to Vietnam, and that's why. He was a cold wall in the sky. The year was 1964, in the land of the sliding door.

My CO Captain Big Joe didn't care if

I live or die, it took me 38

Years to understand

Why...all because

A Korean girl

had caught my eye,

and I had refused to deny.

'Twas a Buffalo Soldier and

A Cold Wall

In the Sky.

(A "water buffalo" is a 400-gallon capacity water trailer for transporting water tot eh field by the Army,)

*Bid Joe became a four-star general.

Where Did Pride Go?

Some of us work our butts off to build a fine machine. And with some of us, it doesn't mean a thing. They come to work all grumpy and mean, and a fine machine don't mean a thing.

I install the bezel, that is my trade, and I hate it when people who build the bezel think they have it made in the shade. I give them a chance to correct mistakes when they're made. And at the end of the line, it appears that their job is fine when it's really me who's lyin'. Most of the time, their job is not fine, I cover their mistakes in time, but from now on, I'll be drawing the line, the repair line.

Mistakes should not increase. They should decline in a year's time!

I hate it when people scratch the bezels and don't care where they are laid. They don't care how the car is made. With some people, they have no pride inside and no self-esteem. They think they can shoot screws looking with the left eye, while the right reads magazines. How can you build a fine machine while reading a magazine?

Give us a break! We come to work to make a paycheck, you come to work a fake a check!

It seems as if you don't want to build this machine, if your paycheck is late, you can look ream. Do you just want the green? Yea, you just want the green. Most of us have self-esteem and want the green. Most of us have self-esteem and want to build this fine machine. When you're reading a magazine, you'll pick up a grey bezel, when it should be green it becomes another mistake, you make that the end of the line hasn't seen.

What Is Your Name, And Your Claim

to Fame?

It was really a shame; his premiums were paid in vain. To them it was just a game, what a shame. Well, Jr. is my name, and my daddy's name was the same. You took his money for a policy and it didn't mean a thing. When I was a little boy, I could not sing, but I could make a guitar twang and this is one song I will sing, 'cause it's a rip-off game and Mutual of Oma is your name.

Your claim to fame will be for unpaid claims. You don't have it made in the shade this story is about how accidental "bed rest" was made...

Black Slade.

EDITOR'S CHOICE AWARD

Presented to:

WILEY WHITFIELD, JR.

December 2003,
For Outstanding Achievement in Poetry.

Presented by P
oetry.com and the International Library of Poetry.

36 Hrs. to Live and Die

I've had seven long years to cry. That's how long it's taken me to say goodbye. And to talk about my daddy and why did he die.

He fell down a flight a step, that's why. And some other reasons not to deny. I'll tell you why.

His death was really an accident, but the 'mutual' says that's a lie. They say his death certificate states "natural cause," that's why. And that's no lie.

They said his autopsy stated heart attack, and that's a fact. And my mother's claim, forget that. So, after seven years and no reply, I decided to try.

This is what I had to say…in my way. My father was 79 years old, and the whole truth is not told. It's true he had a weak heart, but his mind and body were strong. When they said he fell down 3 steps, they were wrong. It was 13 steps, and he was strong.

They didn't check him good cause what they did, no fool would. He had fallen down 13 steps! Not 3. They said his heart didn't need to be monitored and they would put him on "bed rest" instead…36 hrs. Later, he was dead…in his bed.

They misdiagnosed his condition from the very beginning, you see? It was 13 steps, not 3, so they treated him for a minor fall when it was a major fall from the bottom of 13 steps up to the hall.

His autopsy also states, and the mutual refuses to related that "bed rest" contributed to the cause! Therefore, when they misdiagnosed his state, they put him on "bed rest" by mistake! Bed rest, by accident, was the cause. The shock, from such a fall, his heart hadn't time to recuperate from it all.

His heart should have been monitored and exercised to a degree. My mother tried to make them see. What he didn't need was to sleep. His heart needed time to rebuild, so he was accidentally killed.

The Mutual of Oma has written twice to my mother, and they refuse to address "bed rest."

The accidental bed rest, they want my mother to forget that. If my father had put himself on bed rest, I could accept that. But these were medically trained individuals who did what they did through neglect.

Therefore, his accident policy is liable, it seems to me, they don't want to see. All insurance companies are required to settle claims speedily and in good faith. It's stated in the insurance regulations in order to regulate! So Mutual of Oma, where is your faith?

To the Mutual. His heart attack was not by natural cause if it was assisted by two previous accidents.

The fall down the stairwell

Prescribing bed rest instead of a monitor exercise.

When an Accidental Death Policy

Does Not Pay

Two accidents preceded my father's death, the two accidents were connected, and they contributed to him having a "Pulmonary Embolism" while he slept in his bed after having been put on bed rest by mistake by the paramedics who attended to him after he had fallen down a flight of stairs leading to his basement. I believe the first mistake made by the paramedics, is when they wrote in their report that he had fallen down 3 or 4 steps, and they next recommended that he be put on bed rest. His autopsy report stated that the bed rest contributed to the cause of his death. His insurance company Mutual of Omaha refused to pay. They say he died from a heart attack; therefore, their accidental death policy does not have to pay.

It is my contention and belief that his policy is liable for this reason:

My father, Wiley Whitfield Sr., was 79 years old; he fell down a flight of stairs consisting of 13 steps, not 3 or 4 reported in the paramedic's report. They treated him for a minor fall when it was actually a major fall. My mother requested that he be taken to the hospital for observation, and her request was denied. Bed rest was recommended. Had he been taken to the hospital, his heart would have been exercised and monitored to some degree, and he would not have died in his sleep.

Wiley Whitfield, on behalf of Evelyn Whitfield

Turn the Other Cheek

If the police slaps up, turn the other cheek, when "He" said turn the other cheek, "He" meant it to be for certain people. If my wife slaps me, I turn the other cheek; if my mother or father slaps me, I would turn the other cheek; if my sone or daughter slaps me I would turn the other cheek; if my best friend slaps me, I would turn the other cheek. And for brothers and sisters in Christ I would turn the other cheek.

A Double Standard

Michael is supposed to be innocent until proved guilty, so why is he in handcuffs for the whole world to see and the "…priest go free? If he goes to jail…the priest cans go to hell. (When their shoes fit)

Illegally Blind

A law degree does not
Guarantee that one can see.
You can have a law degree
And still can't see.

The Last Cowboy

I was peeping around the corner of our house with one eye. I was searching for my brother who was hiding from me. After 'bout two seconds had passed, I heard the crack sound of his rifle and felt a pain in my eye. The BB had stuck in his eye socket about a fourth of an inch from the center of my eyeball…

I pulled it out and the scar had remained. We were playing cowboys and Indians.

The Hangman's Noose

When someone cut him loose,
He still had on, the hangman's noose…
It was around his neck tied loose.

Inspirations

James and Marvin Jackson (East St. Louis, IL)

Carol Webb (Cahokia High School)

Marvin Tapley (Cahokia High School)

Susan Hagen (US Army)

Lori Orielly (US Army)

Lt. Vernon Anderson (Winner of the Medal of Honor)

Archie and Mary Watts (East St. Louis, IL)

John Hendrix (New York Life)

Cpt. Nannini (US Army) Italy

Emmet Till

Wilfred C. Gleason, Poet

Clifford Warren USA

Dave Trina TAB

Alex

Shelley

Harold

Rob

Broshelle*

John Robinson Coach/Teacher

Chas and Margaret Wren

Ruth and Blake

Kim Jin Tae-Korea

The Cannon Family

Ann Mulholland

Eddie Golliday

Jimmie Golliday

Norvel Ward

Rosie and Ted Gaten

Mike

Mira dn Dace

Jim Funk

Cedrick Hemphil

Roy

Bev

Dennis Patterson

Shirley

Eddie Brown

Joe Broadshaw 1st Sgt.

Lela and Wayne, Italy

Gladys Whigham

Dr. St. Eve and staff

Hon. Me. Price

Theodis Collins Family

Al Crawford

Cornielson Family, Russell & Tammy

Jerry – "Sgt. Mai"

Dean

Jean

"Tom"

Ben

Gary

John

Judy Carpenter*

Cheryl Penske*

New Life Bap. Ch.

Mitchum – Korea

Clinton – Korea

Kenneth Delaney

Robert Perez

Nick Jaramillo

James Wade

Fred Woods

Tony & Kim Bean

Irma and Al

Judy Blackwell

Terry Blackwell

Kim Blackwell

Leroy Crisp

Juan and Mercedes

Rob and Terry

Deak Riviera

Brenda & John

Amanda, "Off the Line" IP.

Andrea

Boddy and Debbie Ogen

Barb and Clyde

"Tracy""

Janet*

"Kevin and Lisa"

"Sheila and Todd"

"Debbie" Barb

Inella

Dawn

Millie

Dave

Tina

Cindy

Clarence, Forman

Arcliese, U.S.A.

"T.J."

James

Bill, "hall of Fame Boxing"

Pat

Kenneth Eugene

"Grace"

Lenny

Cynthis

Dorothy

Shanta

Trudy Johnston – Canada

Chas Riley

Stewart

Eric Winfield, Forman

David Nibbs

Kathy and Joe Springer

Joan Shaw – Gar. Sch.

Willie

Karen and Red Italy

Miro- Italy

Doug

Cherie

Shirley Luster

Wn Yarbrough

Mack Parker

Choi Hun Soo-Korea

"Angel"

Jessie Rice

Kelley Robin*

Homer

Jeff and Kim

Cenola M.

Mark

Thomas Ward, S.C.

Neal

Brad

Logan, G.S.

Gn J.S. Owens

Frank Kowalski

Carolyn Whitaker

"Rhonda"

Kathy"

"Karen

" Katey

"Sandy"

Julia*

Carol and Jim

"Judy"

Chris and Erica

Cindy and Chuck

John and Diane

Donna

Dana, Truck Plant

Deni – Q. Control

Smithton PO.

Mel, Forman

Rosebud and Laura

"Linda S."

Walter

Bamberg, Germany

Shawn

Wanda

Valerie

John and Pam

The Lacy Brothers

"Danny G"

Deloris

Tim, "FSB"

"Danny G"

Deloris

Tim, "FSB"

"Danny Boy"

Ralph

Lawrence Taylor

Lori Kleekamp

Scotty

Deniece

Billy

Cheryl

Frank and Patsy

The Kelso Family – Italy

Sharon

Janice *

Diane

Brian

Jackie

Don

Zeke

"Mother Teresa"

How Do I Say Thanks

Merci Beaucoup
Arigato
Grazie Mille
Danke Shurn
Muchas Gracias
Comopsumnida
And thank you"Jesus"
The blessed name of
The Lord.

In Loving Memory Of

Mr. Wiley Whitfield, Sr.
1912 – 1992

Wednesday, February

19, 1992 7:00 P.M

NEW LIFE MISSIONARY BAPTIST CHURCH
5401 Market Avenue

Centreville, Illinois 62207
REVEREND CODIE JOHNSON, Officiating.

Mr. Wiley Whitfield, Sr., started his life's journey on November 27, 1912, the youngest of ten children born to the union of Eddie and Mary (Costello) Whitfield in Tugaloo. Mississippi.

His mother died when he was only eight years old, thus laying the foundation for his tenacious spirit. He survived many hardships and obstacles.

At the age of fourteen, he moved to Saint Louis, where he worked for ARMOUR & COMPANY. There, he became a master butcher. Later he worked at KREY PACKING COMPANY, from which he retired— after working for 50 years in the industry.

On August 21, 1944, he was joined by his partner for life, Miss Evelyn Louise Rogers, in Holy Matrimony. Together they brought forth eleven children.

Mr. Whitfield believed in working hard, saying, giving, and spending wisely. He labored on a farm for several years while continuing his employment. He and his wife acquired properties and provided housing for many people in Alorton, Centerville, and East Saint Louis.

Wiley professed hope in Christ in 1957 and united with the PILGRIM REST MISSIONARY BAPTIST CHURCH. In 1959, he helped organize and found the NEW LIFE MISSIONARY BAPTIST CHURCH, where he served faithfully as a deacon, trustee, and choir member until his demise.

Mr. Whitfield was well-known and respected throughout the community. His favorite past times were working, reading the Bible, storytelling, playing checkers, and matching wits. He thoroughly enjoyed a good conversation with his friends, but most of all, he enjoyed sharing thoughts of wisdom and inspiration with his children and grandchildren.

He finished his journey and departed this life on February 14, 1992. He leaves to cherish his memory, his loving, devoted wife and partner. Evelyn, University City, Missouri; six sons, Kenneth Eugene Allen, Centreville, Illinois. Wiley Whitfield, Jr., Belleville, Illinois, Reverend Ronal Whitfield, Houston, Texas, Michael Whitfield, Centerville, Illinois, Anthony Whitfield, Jr., Belleville, Illinois, Reverend Ronal Whitfield, Houston, Texas, Micheal Whitfield, Centerville, Illinois, Anthony Whitfield, Los Angeles, California and Tyrone Whitfield, Houston, Texas; five daughters, Mrs. Joe (Gwendolyn) Brunner, Saint Louis County, Missouri, Mrs. Miguel (Gwendolyn) Brunner, Saint Louis County, Missouri, Mrs. Miguel (Paulette) Black, Houston, Texas, Miss Maloney Whitfield, Los Angeles, California, Mrs. Howard (Wilma)

Walker, University City, Missouri and Mrs. Cordell Doss, Berkely, Missouri; one brother, Roscoe Whitfield; one sister, Mrs. Marcus (Jennie) Tweed, Sr., brother East Saint Louis, Illinois; four son-in-law, four daughters-in-law, thirty-three, grandchildren, twelve great-grandchildren, a host of dear nieces, nephews, cousins, neighbors, friends, church family; special niece, bonnie Harris and play daughter, Ethel Kindrell.

Acknowledgements

The Whitfield Family wishes to sincerely thank each of you for your prayers, cards, telegrams, florals, condolences and other expressions of sympathy during our bereavement. We shall remain forever grateful to the Lord for you and your many kind and thoughtful deeds and expressions.

Honorary Pallbearers

Micheal Whitfield	Kenneth Allen
Tyrone Whitfield	Ronald Whitfield
Anthony Whitfield	David Robinson
Wiley Whitfield, Jr.	Jason Whitfield
Mark Robins	Anthony K. Whitfield

ACTIVE PALLBEARERS

Hayes Johnson	James Ross
Dwight Whitfield	Walter Shaw

A TRIBUTE TO DADDY

Strong FaithKeen-Witted Courageous HonestBrilliant Mind IntegrityReliableShrewd Businessmen GenerosityFearlessHard-Working ConsistentDependableOut-Spoken ProtectorProviderWise DignityDistinctionTough

1.Kenneth . . . ."Dad , thanks for not being a - butcher...........................stepfather to me, but being singer........................... a good father"

2. Wiley, Jr . . . . " Dad, you always said, 'As a -insurance man thinks in hear, so is he'. This is a -salestreasure that I will always follow. -musicianToday is the first day of the rest of my life – my best friend died yesterday," (2/14/92)

3.Ronald . . . . " You always said you wanted --pastor   to live and die without suffering or -businessmanbeing burdensome to others… andso you did."

4.Gwen. . . . . "The world was your classroom. -Registered NurseLife your teacher. You learned -ministerwell, passed it on to others, then -singer/composergraduated with Honors." -musician -pastor's wife

5.Paulette . . . . "You made us believe that with God, - freelance commercial artist we could run through a troop and leap over a wall (even the girls). Thanks Dad, is   last leap is for you."

6. Micheal. . . . . "One that never said you loved us, -laborbut showed it everyday." -artist -musician - entrepreneur

Captain Jack" and the Songs of Back Slade…Off the Line

7. Maloney. . . . ."Dad, you just weren't Black and - Marketing Executive Proud, but you moved from pride to purpose."

8. Wilma . . . . "I love you daddy for thc many -singerconversations that helped shape the -composer course of my life." -musician -minister -Entrepreneur

9. Antony . . . . "I gave you flowers while you could -Retail Marketing smell them."

10. Tyrone. . . . ."I often heard you tell others, 'I -computer analystdidn't send my family to church. I took them'. I'm grateful for that – it has taught me to do the same."

11. Tessa. . . . . "Dad, you often talked about the 'Great -Registered Dental Hygienst 'Black Men' in History when all along -composeryou were simply describing your own -singercharacter. Here's to your legacy."

You lived your life.
You walked the walk.
You demonstrated your faith
You left your footprints
Too big for us to fill.
But we know we don't have to
Because you taught us
To make our Own.

Thank you, Dad

Interment

Sunset Gardens of Memory Cemetery Millstadt, Illinois
NASH IN CHARGE